Corinne Tobias
corinneatobias@gmail.com
www.wakeandbakecookbook.com
www.facebook.com/wakeandbakecookbook

Ordering Information:
Wholesale pricing is available on quantity purchases by dispensaries, retail outlets, bookstores, etc.
For details, contact the author at the email address above or call (970) 260-6590.

Printed in the United States of America

Tobias, Corinne
Wake & Bake : a cookbook / Corinne Tobias ; with Aja Kolinski.
p. 104

ISBN 978-0-615-93812-7

First Edition

10 9 8 7 6 5 4 3 2 1

In loving memory

Of the outmoded prohibition laws

Of prisons filled with nonviolent offenders convicted of cannabis related charges

*Of chronically or fatally ill citizens denied access to an
effective organic drug without harmful side effects*

Of young men and women with felony records for victimless crimes

Of misspent law enforcement budgets...

Rest in Peace.

This book is dedicated to the 48 states left to go

and to Nate.

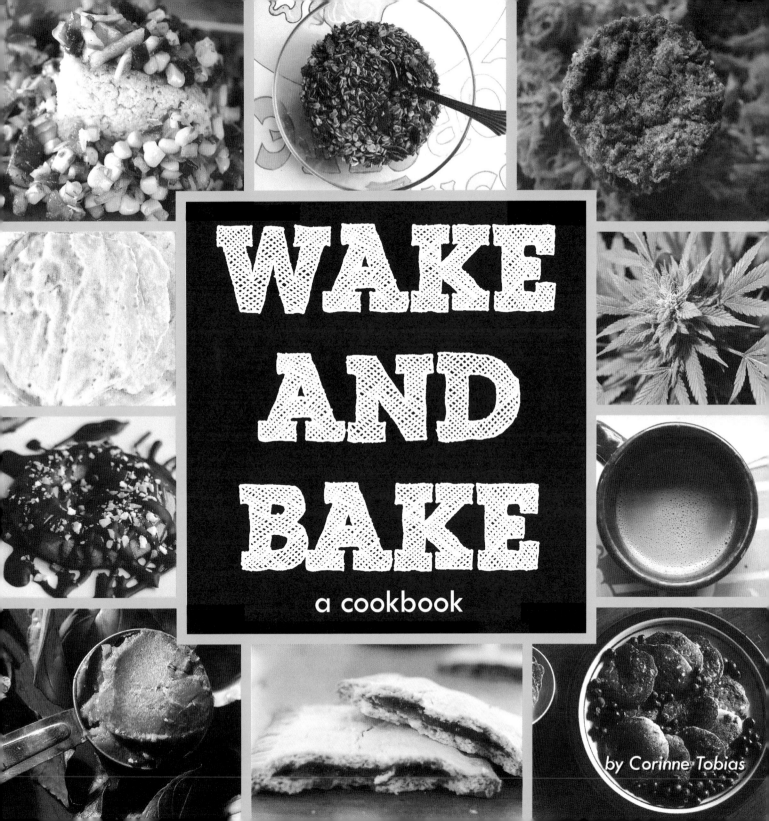

WAKE AND BAKE

a cookbook

by Corinne Tobias

TABLE OF CONTENTS

Introduction 1

Green Monsta Oil Tutorial 6

Cereals 10

Sweet Breakfast 15

Savory Breakfast 22

Muffins 31

Cupcakes 39

Cookies 44

Pies & Things 53

Sweet Munchies 59

Salty Munchies 65

Hippie Shakes 70

Drinks & Coffee Creamers 74

Frostings & Stuff 79

Chocolates 86

Ingredient Conversion Chart 92

Thank you 93

Index 94

WELCOME TO WAKE & BAKE !

This is a cookbook designed with everyone in mind. Well, it's designed for anyone who has a mind to put cannabis in his or her food and eat it.

Are you one of us?

Good! Let's get started. A few things:

1. I don't use dairy or wheat products, so the recipes are mostly gluten free and vegan. Don't let that scare you non-gluten-free-veganoids because...
2. ALL of these recipes can be baked using conventional flours and ingredients (there's a conversion chart in the back to sub out any of the ingredients). We believe in equal opportunity baking! The ingredient substitutions are mainly 1 for 1, so it's not complicated. Just check the chart if you're planning on using something different.
3. As a home cook, I wanted to make a cannabis cookbook for other home cooks, even ones without any kitchen experience. I tried to make the recipes as simple as possible, without complicated tools or rare ingredients. I hope that this shines through and that everyone is able to use this cookbook to make amazing edibles in their own homes with ease.
4. We always love feedback so we can get better at what we do. Please contact us at facebook.com/wakeandbakecookbook with any questions or comments.

Lovely. Now that we got that out of the way, I'd like to thank you for picking this book up and putting it in your hands. Wake & Bake, our very first cookbook, supports an independent publishing project that we would love to continue working on. Thank you, thank you, thank you for supporting creativity.

Much Love,
Corinne and The Wake & Bake Team

TOOLS

Like I said, this is a cookbook made for home cooks, so I don't use any fancy shmancy gadgets that the average kitchen wouldn't be stocked with. However, there are a few things that make life so much easier if you're going to cook edibles at home.

I use the following in this book:
- Food processor
- Blender or an
  Immersion Blender
- Crockpot
- Rolling Pin
- Parchment Paper
- Cheesecloth
- Round Cookie Cutters
- Cupcake Liners
- Measuring Cups/Spoons
- A Whisk!

In many instances, you can rough it and use another appliance or method. Whatever you decide to use, always use your noggin.

CHOOSING A GF FLOUR

There are lots of different options when choosing a gluten free flour or flour blend. I tried to find a flour blend that was affordable, widely available and that had good texture and flavor.

I landed on Bob's Red Mill Gluten Free All Purpose Flour Blend for almost all of the recipes. I could find it in many grocery stores and also found it in bulk sections. It has a great texture and Bob doesn't include any gums in the mix (see below). This mix is bean based though, so anything no-bake is no bueno because it will taste like beans. I like Pamela's Artisan Blend for those recipes.

I used a few prepackaged mixes as well (I've never had better cornbread than the Bob's Redmill mix), so you'll see that in 2 or 3 of the recipes.

Feel free to use conventional wheat flour, spelt flour, your own GF flour blend, or experiment with other mixes.

ON GUMS

I don't use any Guar or Xanthan gums in this book. Why?

1. I wanted to see if you could bake delicious gluten free and vegan goodies without them. You can. And the texture of everything in this book turned out great in the test kitchen. I used tapioca starch as a thickener and binder for a few things and it did the trick.

2. Xanthan gum is made from fermented sugar and a specific strain of bacteria, so it can only be made in a test tube. It is also used as a laxative. It can cause gas and bloating (which is a sign that your digestive system is piiiissed at what you put in it). No thank you. It hasn't been studied much, but it can reportedly do some crazy stuff in large doses, so I'd rather just leave it out.

3. Guar gum, although made from a seed, reportedly has similar side effects (bloating, gas, indigestion).

4. I didn't know enough about either of these to feel confident in using and recommending them, especially if you're using these edibles as a treatment for disease or pain.

Now, you might be asking yourself why a cookbook filled with sugar and oil is concerned about small amounts of binding agents and what they do to your digestive system. Don't ask questions. Just bake.

MAKING A FLAAXY EGG

It's way easier than making your own chicken egg, especially if you don't happen to be a chicken.

**1 Flaaxy Egg =
1 T Ground Flax + 3 T Water**

Whisk or fork until combined and set aside for a few minutes before use.

A NOTE ABOUT THE GREEN MONSTA OIL

The Green Monsta Oil in this book is an infused coconut oil that is incredibly flavorful and has a good deal of saturated fat for the THC and other cannabinoids to bind to. The strength of the oil depends on the quality of trim that you use. Each "Stoney Serving" in this book = 1 Tablespoon of GM Oil. Always test your oil strength in advance by shmearing a small amount on a piece of toast.

Green Monsta Tutorial

TOOLS

- Crockpot

- Cheesecloth

- Small Strainer

- 1 Quart or 2 Pint Jars

INGREDIENTS

- 2 ½ Cups Trim or Fresh Prunings

- 3 Cups Coconut Oil

TIME

- 4-6 hours

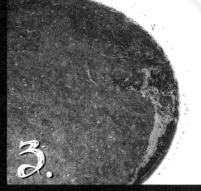

STEP 1

Measure your greens. You can use fresh prunings or dry trim.

STEP 2

Measure coconut oil. You'll want to have enough oil to cover the trim or prunings. I use about 3 Cups Coconut Oil to 2 ½ Cups of Trim.

STEP 3

In a crockpot, melt Coconut Oil on low heat. Add prunings or trim to the oil and stir. *My crockpot gets pretty hot on the low setting, so I switch between low and warm. If the oil starts to smoke, it's definitely too hot. Turn the heat down or off until cool, and then return it to the lowest setting. Stir every half hour or so. After several hours of heating and steeping, turn off the crockpot and allow the oil to cool before moving onto the next step.

STEP 4

Set up your strainer so it fits snugly in a container. Line with a large piece of cheesecloth.

STEP 5

Pour plant matter and oil into the strainer slowly.

STEP 6

Using a string or twist tie, gather the cheesecloth around the plant matter and secure.

STEP 7

SQEEEEEEEEEEEEZE that shit.*Save this satchel to make High Chai (opposte page)

STEP 8

Pour oil into jars and place in the refrigerator until solid. Seal jars with lids.

STEP 9

Store in refrigerator or in a cool dark place.

STEP 10

Spread it on toast. Make Wake & Bake recipes with it. Rub it on your achy body parts. Just open it up and sniff it every time you walk by. Every time.

High Chai
the resourceful way

I like to make a batch of Chai after making a batch of Green Monsta Oil, using the leftover plant material in the bag of cheesecloth.

The spiced flavor pairs well with the strongly flavored oil. This recipe was based on what I had on hand when making a batch of Green Monsta Oil was finished. You can include whole Allspice and Fresh Ginger (recommended) if those are in your cupboard when you make a batch.

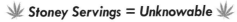 *Stoney Servings = Unknowable*

INGREDIENTS

- 6 Cups Water
- 1.5 t Garam Masala
- 3 t Cinnamon
- 10 Cardamom Pods (crushed)
- 6 whole Cloves (crushed)

- 3-4 T Black Tea
- ½ Cup Nutmilk (Plus more, for taste)
- Bag of leftover plant material from Green Monsta Oil (See tutorial step 7)

METHOD

1. Add all spices to water over medium high heat and boil for 10-15 minutes.

2. Reduce heat to medium-low. Add Bag of Leftover Plant Material and Black Tea.

3. Steep for 10-15 minutes.

4. Allow to cool enough so you can pull the cheesecloth bag out of the water and sqeeze out the remaining oil and tea.

5. Strain all spices. Add Nutmilk and whisk insanely or hit it with an immersion blender to emulsify the oil).

6. When reheating, mix chai with Nutmilk (as desired), & 1 t of liquid sweetener per serving. Re-emulsify as necessary.

CEREALS

Weedies

Want to slam dunk your day? Oh... Then you probably shouldn't eat weed food in the morning.

Want to go to the park and wander around? These are fuel for you!

This Wake & Bake Breakfast o' Champions was reported to be, "the best homemade thing ever," by a taste tester. Booyah.

🌿 **8 Stoney Servings** 🌿
about ½ cup = 1 Stoney Serving

INGREDIENTS

- 2 Cups Oats
- Pinch o' Salt
- ¼ Cup Sunflower Seeds
- ¼ Cup Walnuts or Pecans
- ¼ Cup Coconut Shavings (or other dried fruit)
- ½ Cup Green Monsta Oil (Melted)
- ½ Cup Brown Sugar
- ¼ Cup Maple Syrup
- Huge Pinch of Cinnamon and/or Nutmeg

METHOD

1. Preheat oven to 350°
2. In a large bowl, combine all ingredients. Mix!
3. Spread in a thin even layer on cookie sheet.
4. Stir every 15 minutes.
5. Bake until golden.
6. Chill totally. Serve with cold nut milk.

Stooonie Crisp Cereal

Do you remember in the 90's when they started turning everything into cereal?

Chocolate chip cookies? Cereal!

Cinnamon toast? Ceareal!

Reeses Pieces? Cereal!

S'mores? Cereal!

A guy who survives on the blood of virgins? Ceeereal!

Correction: Count Chocula has been kickin it since the 70's. But still...

I think you get the point.

This recipe is a testament to hippie ingenuity. In order to make these ridiculously cute cookies, you need something like a pastry bag. Why not make your own?

I used an old gallon baggie and a frosting tip. But if you don't have either of those things on hand, use your noggin. I'm sure you can come up with something to turn it into... cereal!

INGREDIENTS

- 1 1/3 Cups GF Flour
- ½ t Baking Powder
- ½ t Salt
- 2/3 Cup Mini Chocolate Chips
  (we used the Good Life brand)
- ½ Cup Sugar
- ½ Cup Melted Green Monsta Oil
- 1 Egg or 1 Flaaxy Egg
- 4 t Vanilla
- 6-10 T Nut Milk

8 Stoney Servings

METHOD

1. Preheat oven to 325°
2. Line cookie sheets or baking pans with parchment paper.
3. Mix Flour, Baking Powder and Salt. Whisk!
4. Pour Chocolate Chips into small bowl. Toss with 1 T of Flour mix.
5. Add Sugar to Flour Mix. Stir!
6. Add Monsta Oil, Egg/Flaaxy Egg, and Vanilla. Stir!
7. Add 6 T Nut Milk. Stir!
8. Add bowl of Chocolate Chips. Stir!
9. Add Nut Milk 1 Tablespoon at a time until dough is soft enough to be piped.
10. Pipe dime-nickel sized cookies, about one inch apart.
11. Flatten tops with wet fingers.
12. Bake 10 Minutes until golden around the edges and crunchy in your mouth.
13. Allow to cool 10 minutes.
14. Cereal!

Shake -N- Bake Granola

There's nothing better than waking up to a bowl of homemade granola. If that granola happens to be infused with one of the most impactful herbs known to man, well, I guess that kinda trumps everything. Granola can seem like a massive undertaking, but it's incredibly easy after you do it just once. We promise... You've got this in the bag.

INGREDIENTS

- 3 Cups Oats
- 1 Cup Green Monster Oil
- ½ Cup Honey
- ½ Cup Cashews
- ½ Cup Walnuts
- ½ Cup Sunflower Seeds

16 Stoney Servings

OPTIONAL
Add ¼ cup dried fruit

SUBSTITUTIONS
GF: Use GF Oats

Vegan:
Sub Agave for Honey

Less Stoney:
½ C Green Monsta
and ½ C Coconut Oil

METHOD

1. Preheat oven to 325°.
2. Chop walnuts and cashews to desired size, or leave them big and chunky.
3. Combine all ingredients. Mix.
4. Spread in a layer on a greased cookie sheet.
5. Stir every 15 minutes.
6. Bake until golden.

SWEET BREFAS

"Some of my finest hours have been spent on my back veranda, smoking hemp and observing as far as my eye can see."

- Thomas Jefferson

Ganja Flapjacks

Have you ever spent a day eating only pancakes? It's okay. There's always today.

Today, make a batch of these (silver dollar style) and see if you want to eat anything else.

There's just one Stoney Serving in a batch of flapjacks. To up the intensity, serve with Ganashish (for chocolate chip pancakes) or make some Ganjam (1/2 cup berries in a small pot over low heat until mushy. Add 1-3 T melted Green Monsta Oil, and 1-2 T Maple Syrup. Mash until combined).

 1 Stoney Serving

INGREDIENTS

- 1 Cup GF/Dairy Free Pancake Mix
- 1 Flaaxy Egg
  (1T Ground Flax + 3T Water)
  or 1 Egg
- ¾ Cup Water
- 1 T Green Monsta Oil (melted)
- ¼ Cup Berries or Mini Chocolate Chips

METHOD

1. Mix Flaaxy Egg and set aside.

2. Combine all ingredients and mix until lumps disappear.

3. Pour ¼ Cup Batter onto a lightly oiled, preheated, pan.

4. When the top is all bubbly, flip and cook the other side.

5. Eat immediately, or store in the freezer for later.

Pot Tarts

I know what you're thinking. Pot tart is the cleverest pun you've ever heard.

If you're a gluten free veganite, being able to reincorporate toaster pastries into your balanced breakfast of other toaster pastries, totally feels like a new beginning. Birds will sing. Clouds will part. Roomates and lovers will flock to the kitchen. Then roomates might turn into lovers; lovers into roomates.

Be careful. Cohabitation can become complicated. Lucky for you, these Pot Tarts are not. Serve them with Vavavanilla frosting or eat them right out of the oven.

INGREDIENTS

- 1 ¼ Cups GF Flour
- Dash Salt
- 1/3 Cup Sugar
- 4 T Green Monsta Oil (melted)
- ½ t vanilla
- ¼ Cup Nut Milk (room temp)
- Jam or Cinnamon Sugar Filling

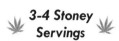

3-4 Stoney Servings

OPTIONAL

Top with Vavavanilla Frosting (pg 85)

Try any seedless jam

Sprinkles

METHOD

1. Preheat oven to 350° F. Line a pan or cookie sheet with parchment paper and put aside.
2. Combine flour, salt & sugar. Whisk!
3. Add melted Green Monsta Oil, vanilla and milk.
4. Mix and knead dough until smooth.
5. Turn dough out onto a sheet of parchment paper and cover with another sheet of parchment paper.
6. Roll dough out to 1/8" thick.
7. Cut into Pot Tart sized rectangles and carefully move rectangles onto the prepared cookie sheet.
8. Spread jam or filing in an even layer.
9. Cover the rectangles with the other rectangles.
10. Press with the flat edge of the fork to seal.
11. Bake until golden with darker edges.

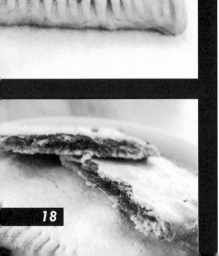

French Toast Casserole

Bread Pudding + French Toast + Strusel Topping + Cannabis Infused Coconut Oil
= The French Toast Casserole

This casserole is best of all worlds. It's probably the best breakfast in every planet on every dimension of the universe. It defies time and space.

It does take up some time and space in your fridge while the bread soaks in all of the sweet goodness, so prepare it the night before or a few hours before you plan on serving it.

INGREDIENTS

FRENCH TOAST CASSEROLE
- ¾ Cup Nut Milk
- 3 T Ground Flax
- 1 T Brown Sugar
- 1 T Maple Syrup
- 1 t Vanilla
- 1 t Cinnamon
- 5-6 Slices of Bread (GF or not)

STRUSEL TOPPING
- ¼ Cup GF Flour
- ¼ Cup Brown Sugar
- ¼ t Cinnamon
- 3-4 T Green Monsta Oil (cold)

 *3-4 Stoney Servings*

METHOD

FRENCH TOAST CASSEROLE
1. Tear or cut Slices of Bread into 2 inch chunks and layer in an 8x8 or Bread Loaf Pan depending on desired thickness.
2. Combine Nut Milk, Ground Flax, Brown Sugar, Maple Syrup, Vanilla and Cinnamon.
3. Pour Nut Milk Mix over bread and mix in with your fingers.
4. Refrigerate, and let soak for at least a few hours. Overnight is best.
5. Preheat oven to 350°.

STRUSEL TOPPING
1. Mix Flour, Sugar, and Cinnamon.
2. Cut in Green Monsta Oil
3. Pour Strusel Topping over Bread and bake for about 45 minutes, or until the strusel turns golden and crumbly.

Cinnamon Rollies

If you ever want to impress someone, bust out some homemade cinnamon rolls. If you ever want to impress someone, and have them forget all about it in a few minutes, bust out these Cinnamon Rollies. These are so sweet, warm, and comforting. Perfect for holiday gatherings (please don't drug your grandparents), or cold winter mornings, followed by afternoons in which you misplace your car keys six times.

🌿 *6-8 Stoney Servings* 🌿

INGREDIENTS

- 1 2/3- 2 Cups Gluten Free All Purpose Flour
- 1 ¼ t Baking Powder
- Dash Salt
- ¼ Cup Pure Cane Sugar
- 6 T Green Monsta Oil
- 1 Large Egg or 1 Flaaxy Egg
- ¼ Cup Nut Milk
- ¼ Cup Coconut Milk
- ¼ Cup Dark Brown Sugar
- 2 T Cinnamon

1. Preheat oven to 350°F.

2. Grease 6-8 wells of a regular twelve-cup muffin tin and set it aside.

3. In a large bowl, place 1 2/3 cups of the Flour, Baking Powder, a dash of Salt, and the Sugar. Whisk.

4. Add 2 T Green Monsta Oil, Egg/Flaaxy Egg, Nut Milk and Coconut Milk. Mix.

5. Knead with floured hands until dough is smooth.

6. Turn the Dough out onto a sheet of flour dusted parchment paper. Place another sheet on top.

7. Roll the dough out in a rectangle until it is about ¼ inch thick.

8. In a separate bowl, mix Brown Sugar, Cinnamon, 4 T of Green Monsta Oil, and a dash of Salt. Mix.

9. Spread the Cinnamon Mixture over the rectangle of dough in an even layer. Leave ½ inch barren around the perimeter.

10. Roll the dough away from you. Get it tight.

11. Slice the roll into rounds at least 1 inch thick.

12. Stuff each roll into the well of a muffin tin.

13. Bake for about 25 minutes, until golden.

14. Let them chill. When they're just warm to the touch, remove rolls from muffin tin and drizzle with warm Vavavanilla Icing.

The Faker Quaker Baker

As far back as I can remember, I could put the hurt on a box of chewy chocolate chip granola bars. Those tiny planks of sticky oats and chocolate chips couldn't compete with my childhood sugar addiction.

Now, I'm a grownup and my sugar addiction is none of anyone's business. But, say I did have a sugar issue, just to make an example, not because there's anything wrong with me (or the New Guinea sweet sap)... Well, these granola bars would keep a real sugar addict from going into withdrawal any time soon.

But not me though, because I don't have a problem with that kind of thing.

INGREDIENTS

- 2 Cups Oats
- ½ Cup Sugar
- ¼ t Salt
- ½ t Cinnamon
- ¼ t Allspice (optional)
- ½ Cup Mini Chocolate Chips
- ½ Cup Sunflower Seeds
- ¼ Cup Coconut Flakes (optional)
- 1/3 Cup Nut Butter
- 6 T Green Monsta Oil (melted)
- ¼ Cup +1-2 T Liquid Sweetner (Maple, Honey, Agave)
- 1 T Water

 6 Stoney Servings

METHOD

1. Preheat oven to 350°. Line a pie plate, 8x8 or 9x13 pan with parchment paper.
2. Process 1/3 cup of the Oats in a blender or food processor until finely ground.
3. In a large bowl, stir together dry ingredients: Ground Oats, Oats, Sugar, Salt, Spices, Nuts/Seeds, Chocolate Chips.
4. Combine wet ingredients: Green Monsta Oil, Liquid Sweetner, Nut Butter, and Water.
5. Add wet to dry. Mix.
6. Press into pie plate or pan.
7. Bake for at least 30 minue, depending on the size pan you use. The edges will turn deep gold when it's ready to go.
8. Divide into six equal parts.

SAVORY BREFAS

Cornbread Brefas

At Wake & Bake headquarters, our Iron Chef competitions look more like American Gladiator competitions. There's generally a lot more wrestling and smack talking than there is actually cooking or plating.

But for this Cornbread Brefas recipe, a plating battle commenced. After cheating immensely, the farmer was declared the winner (to his credit, his did look like a ship parting the seas of Pico De Gallo with a bean waterfall cascading down the back).

This is a really versatile meal idea. The Cornbread is infused with cannabis, so virtually any topping would work, but this Chili Bean and Pico combo was outstanding.

 **5-6 Stoney Servings**

INGREDIENTS

CORNBREAD
- 1 Package Bob's Red Mill Gluten Free Cornbread Mix
- 1 ½ Cups Nut Milk
- 1/3 Cup Green Monsta Oil (Melted)
- 2 Flaaxy Eggs (2T Flax + 6 T Water) or 2 Eggs

PICO DE GALLO
- 6 Roma Tomatoes
- 2 Jalapeños
- 1 Medium Red Onion
- 4 Cloves Garlic
- ½ Bunch Cilantro
- 1 Can Organic Sweet Corn
- Salt & Pepper (to taste)

BEANS
- 1 Can Organic Chili Beans *(heated)*

24

METHOD

CORNBREAD

1. Follow directions on the GF Cornbread Mix, but sub melted Green Monsta Oil for the regular oil.

PICO DE GALLO

1. Cut Romas in half and squeeze out the juice.

2. Remove some or all of the seeds from the Jalepenos.

3. Dice all veggies to ¼ inch chunks.

4. In a large bowl, mix all ingredients.

5. Cover and refrigerate until ready to serve. The flavor gets better after a day or so.

Serve Warm Cornbread with Heated Beans and Pico.

Baked Biscuits

When we'd visit my Mawmaw in Tennessee, she'd almost always make us biscuits and chocolate gravy. It was an 8 am sugar high that I'm not sure you can ever come down from. You'll eventually come down from these biscuits, but probably not until after you rename your cat six times.

And yes. Biscuit is a great cat name.

🌿 **2 Stoney Servings** 🌿
2 Biscuits = 1 Stoney Serving

INGREDIENTS

- 1 Cup GF Flour (Bob's)
- ½ T Baking Powder
- ¼ t Baking Soda
- Dash o' Salt
- 2 T Green Monsta Oil (refrigerated and chopped up)
- ½ Cup Nut Milk + ½ T Apple Cider Vinegar

METHOD

1. Preheat oven to 450°
2. Prepare a baking sheet lined with parchment paper.
3. Whisk together Flour, Baking Powder, Baking Soda and Salt.
4. Using your fingers, mix in cold Green Monsta Oil until it looks like sand.
5. Create a well in the middle of your sand mixture and pour in Almond Milk and Apple Cider Vinegar.
6. Stir until just combined.
7. Turn dough out onto a floured surface, dust top of dough ball with flour, and knead it super super lightly (5-6 times).
8. Form a 1" thick disc with your hands and using a cookie cutter or glass, cut out large biscuits.
9. Place biscuits on prepared backing pan making sure they touch each other.
10. Bake for 10-12 minutes, or until lightly golden.
11. Serve immediately with Coconut Oil & Jam, Gravy or guacamole. These biscuits are best when they're right out of the oven, but you could store them in the fridge for a day or so.

Bullseye Mashed Tater Egg Bake

The Farmer likes the yolk of his eggs to be completely cooked. I'm more of an over easy kind of lady. The beauty of a single serving egg dish? You can please everyone. Or you can skip the approval seeking process and make one just for you. You can make this single serving Egg Bake as a Roasted Veggie Bake (vegan). It's a great way to use up some leftover mashers and/or roasted veggies.

This recipe can be doubled, tripled, quadrupled, and.... uh... made into five times as many servings. Experiment with different tater varieties, herbs and spices when creating the Mashed Potato Mix.

INGREDIENTS

- 1/3-1/2 cup Mashed Sweet Potato

- 1t Green Monsta Oil

- 1 Egg

- Salt & Pepper

1 Stoney Serving
🌿 *(medium)* 🌿

OPTIONAL
Use 1 T of Green Monsta for a Stonier Experience
———
Sriracha.
Always Sriracha.

METHOD

1. Grease one medium ramekin lightly.

2. In a small bowl, mix Mashed Sweet Potato with Green Monsta Oil.

3. Fill ¾ of the ramekin with Mashed Sweet Potato Mix.

4. Bake at 375° about 10-15 minutes, until top starts gettin' golden.

5. Remove ramekin from oven and crack an egg on top of the Sweet Potato Mix.

6. Sprinkle with Salt & Pepper.

7. Place ramekin back in oven and bake until desired yolk solidness.

Roasted Veggie Quiche Meditation

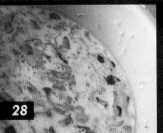

This Quiche crust was a real Biche. It gets the job done, and it tastes fantastic, but it takes some wrangling to get the crust into the pie plate, and it's not the best looking bee in the barrel.

This crust prompted several discussions about perfection, control and anal retentivism, and now... here it is. It will test your spiritual integrity and allow you to look at yourself honestly, seeing how your inner critic plays out in your daily life. Or, if you're not in need of couch therapy, it will hold scrambled eggs into the shape of a pie.

 8 Stoney Servings

INGREDIENTS

- 1 Bell Pepper of Any Color
- ½ Large Onion
- 4 Cloves Garlic
- 1 Med Russet Potato
- 1-2 T Olive Oil
- 1-2 T Herbs (rosemary, thyme, or sage)
- 6 Eggs
- ½ Cup Green Monsta Oil
- ½ t Salt
- 1 Cup Gluten Free All Purpose Flour
- 3-4 T Cold Water

1. Preheat oven to 300°.

2. Chop Bell Pepper, Onion, Garlic and Tater into ½ inch chunks.

3. Toss in olive oil and optional herbs.

4. Roast in oven for 20-30 minutes, stirring occasionally.

5. While veggies are roasting, combine Salt & Flour in a mixing bowl. Whisk.

6. Cut in Green Monsta Oil. Add water.

7. Lightly knead dough.

8. Roll pie crust out to 1/8 inch thickness. See what comes up for you internally. Write it down on a sheet of paper and set it on fire.

9. Do whatever it takes to get the pie crust into the tin. Take three deep breaths and remind yourself that other universes exist. In one of them, you probably are a pie crust. See yourself in the pie crust.

10. Prebake the pie crust for 10 minutes.

11. Scramble Eggs and fold in roasted veggies.

12. Pour into PreBaked pie crust.

13. Bake until golden on top, and until a toothpick or knife comes out clean.

14. Slice... Serve... Transcend...

Tortillas

How do you smuggle weed into your breakfast burrito or morning tacos? Turn the tortilla into your drug mule!

This is an easy way to incorporate cannabis into your breakfast meal without going the sweet route. You can use any GF/Vegan baking mix that has a tortilla recipe on it. I used Pamela's Pizza Crust Mix. You can make these into 10-12 small tortillas or about 6-8 burrito sized tortillas.

Pack that mule, baby. Pack it.

Stoney Servings 5-6
2 Small Flour Tortillas = 1 Stoney Serving

INGREDIENTS

- 1 bag Pamela's GF Pizza Crust Mix
- 2 ¼ t Active Dry Yeast (included in the mix)
- 1/3 Cup Green Monsta Oil
- ¼ t Salt
- 1 Cup Super Warm Water (110°)

OPTIONAL
Serve with nut butter and jelly, refried beans and taters, roasted veggies, etc...

METHOD

1. Combine all ingredients and mix for 30 seconds-1 minute.
2. Cook dough pronto. Do not let it rise.
3. Onto a piece of parchment paper, scoop out dough (heaping ¼ for large tortillas or a little over 1/8 cup for small tortillas).
4. Place another piece of parchment on top and roll out very thin.
5. Heat a large greased skillet over medium heat.
6. Remove the top piece of parchment, and slap the tortilla (dough side down) onto the skillet.
7. As the parchment begins to bubble away from the tortilla, peel it away. Flip to cook the other side.
8. Serve immediately (these dry out quickly and need to be stored in plastic wrap to stay fresh for a day or so).

Eggs in Some Basket

These are totally perfect if you're going hiking or if you have a long day on the farm. These take some prep time and they chill for a while in the oven, so plan ahead. Also, after squeezing hash browns for years by hand and making a recent switch to the cheesecloth method, it's totally worth investing $1.78 in a little cheesecloth.

INGREDIENTS
- 2 Russet Potatoes
- ¼ Cup Green Monsta Oil (melted)
- Salt & Pepper (to taste)
- 4 Eggs

  4 Stoney Servings

METHOD

1. Preheat oven to 350° and grease 4 wells of a jumbo muffin tin or 4 ramekins.
2. Scrub the taters to get soil off.
3. Grate the taters.
4. Squeeze the liquid out of the taters using a piece of cheesecloth or your hands. Get as much liquid out as possible.
5. Add taters to a bowl, mix in the melted Green Monsta Oil.
6. Season with Salt & Pepper.
7. Press taters into the wells of the muffin tin or ramekins. Fill about halfway and allow for a thin layer of taters to come up the sides.
8. Bake for 35-40 minutes.
9. Remove from oven and crack one egg into each cup.
10. Bake until white is set, but yolks are still runny (about 6-10 minutes).

MUFFINS

Fake Bake Carrot Cake Muffins

Did you know that you can turn orange from eating too many carrots? Now that you know, you can lay off your fake tanning regimen and get your supernatural glow from eating a root crop. You're welcome.

These muffins probably won't turn you orange, but they're packing some green, so they will intoxicate you. So wait until they wear off before you rub yourself down with sparkly goo, put on your tiny eyeball goggles, and hop in the old Melanoma charging station.

INGREDIENTS

- 1 Cup Sugar
- ½ Cup Green Monsta Oil (melted)
- 2 Flaaxy Eggs (2T Flax + 6T Water) or 2 Eggs
- 1/4 t Salt
- 1 Cup GF Flour
- ½ t Baking soda
- ½ t Baking Powder
- ½ t Cinnamon
- 1 Cup Grated Carrots

8 Stoney Servings in 12 Muffins
(Pairing with Vavavanilla Icing will make each muffin 1 stoney serving)

OPTIONAL
Vavavanilla Icing (pg 85)
or Dip in melted Green Monsta
then dip in Sugar

METHOD

1. Preheat oven to 350°.
2. Grease the wells of a muffin tin.
3. In a large bowl, mix Sugar, Green Monsta Oil and Flaaxy Eggs/Eggs.
4. In a separate bowl, mix Flour, Salt, Baking Soda, Baking Powder and Cinnamon.
5. Add Flour Mix to Green Monsta Mix. Combine.
6. Fold in Carrots.
7. Scoop batter into prepared muffin tin. 2/3- ¾ full.
8. Bake until edges are golden and toothpick comes out clean.

Johnny Appleseed Muffins

Johnny Appleseed, the American myth and legend who reportedly guerilla gardened North America, was really an inspired but eccentric businessman.

Back in the day, federal law required that new settlers grow fruit trees to establish their permanence. So Johnny went from new settlement to new settlement, growing apple trees from seed wherever he went, selling them to the new settlers as soon as they arrived.

Since apples are never true to seed (meaning if you plant a Fuji seed, you won't get a tree filled with Fujis; you'll get mutants that taste and look completely different), Johnny created an abundance of apple varieties, many of which could only be used to make boozy apple cider.

Johnny never took a wife in this life, believing that he'd be rewarded with two virgins in the afterlife. He planted from seed because he thought that was what god would have wanted. Apparently, god wanted the early colonists to get hammered.

This abundance of alcohol led to the prohibition movement, which led to the empowerment of organized crime. So yeah, you could call Johnny Appleseed the original gangsta. These muffins are for Johnny, in hopes that he's chillin' with his ladies on a cloud somewhere.

- 1 Cup GF Flour
  (+ 1T for coating apples)
- ¾ t Baking Powder
- ¼ t Salt
- 1 t Cinnamon
  (+ ¼ t for coating apples)
- 1 Cup Diced Apples
- ¼ Cup Green Monsta Oil
  (room temp)
- ½ Cup Sugar
- 1 Flaaxy Egg
  (1 T Ground Flax + 3 T Water)
  or 1 Egg
- 1 t Vanilla
- ¼ Cup Nut Milk

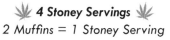
4 Stoney Servings
2 Muffins = 1 Stoney Serving

1. Preheat oven to 375°.
2. Grease 8 wells of a muffin tin, or line with cupcake liners.
3. In a small bowl, toss Diced Apples in extra Cinnamon and Flour.
4. In a medium bowl, combine Flour, Baking Powder, Salt and Cinnamon. Whisk!
5. In a large bowl, Cream Green Monsta Oil and Sugar until smooth.
6. Add Flaaxy Egg/Egg and Vanilla. Mix!
7. Fold in Flour Mix, alternating with Nut Milk. Stir until just combined.
8. Fold in Coated Apples.
9. Scoop dough into wells (¾ full).
10. Bake 25-30 Minutes. Until golden around the edges and toothpick comes out clean.

Mile High Muffins

In 2013, the residents of the great state of Colorado legalized recreational cannabis. Historic? Yes. Awesome? Absolutely.

So make these muffins to celebrate democracy in action. Make them when you meet a fork in the road and have to choose a new way to go.

Make them for freedom's sake.

 *2 Stoney Servings*

OPTIONAL
Make them without the topping for a little less sweetness/stoneyness.

Drizzle with Vavavanilla Icing (pg 85) for more sweetness/stoneyness.

INGREDIENTS

MILE HIGH MUFFIN
- ¾ Cup GF Flour
- ½ t Baking Soda
- Pinch o' Salt
- 1 Small Flaaxy Egg
  (1/2 T Ground Flax + 1 ½ T Water)
- 1 T Monsta Oil (Melted)
- 7 T Nut Milk
- ½ t Vanilla
- ¼ Cup Berries
  (Blueberries/Service Berries)

TOPPING
- 1 T Flour
- 1 T Brown Sugar
- Pinch Cinnamon
- 1 T Green Monsta
  (cold and cut into mini chunks)

1. Preheat oven to 375°.

2. Grease 2 Medium Ramekins.

3. In a large mixing bowl, make Flaaxy Egg and set aside.

4. In a medium mixing bowl, mix Flour, Baking Soda and Salt. Whisk!

5. Add melted Green Monsta Oil, Vanilla, and Nut Milk to Flaaxy Egg. Mix!

6. Slowly add Flour Mix to Monsta Oil Mix. Stir until just combined.

7. Fold in Berries.

8. Fill Ramekins 2/3-3/4 full.

9. Combine Topping Ingredints: Whisk Flour, Brown Sugar, and Cinnamon. Then, using a fork, cut in the chunks of cold Green Monsta Oil.

10. Pour topping on batter and sprinkle with a few berries.

11. Bake 25-30 minutes, until golden and toothpick comes out clean.

Nanner Muffins

Are you ready to have your mind blown?

Bananas grow on one of the largest grass varieties on the planet. A banana tree = one clump of grass.

Next time you see a banana tree, have your very own "Honey, I Shrunk The Kids" moment and pretend you've been blasted with a shrink gun and you're standing next to a huge blade of grass. You totally are.

These Nanner Muffins are also filled with "grass". But that kind of grass is actually an herb.

Has your mind been blown, or just confused?

Well, get your mind right with these Nanner Muffins. Then it'll be way easier to envision a shrunken version of yourself standing next to giant banana grass.

INGREDIENTS

- ½ Cup Overripe Nanners (mashed)
- ¾ Cup + 2 T GF Flour
- ½ Cup + 2T Sugar
- ½ T Baking Powder
- ½ t Cinnamon
- ½ t Nutmeg
- Pinch o' Salt
- ¼ Cup Green Monsta (melted)
- ¼ Cup Warmed Nut Milk
- 2 T Brown Sugar
- ½ T Vanilla

 4 Stoney Servings

OPTIONAL
Extra Green Monsta Oil (melted) and Sugar for dipping

METHOD

1. Preheat oven to 400°.
2. Grease a muffin tin, or place liners in muffin tin wells.
3. In a small bowl, mash your Nanners.
4. In a large mixing bowl, combine Flour, Sugar, Baking Powder, Cinnamon, Nutmeg, and Salt.
5. In another bowl, combine Melted Green Monsta Oil, Warmed Nut Milk, Brown Sugar, and Vanilla.
6. Add Wet mix to Flour mix & stir until just combined (too much stirring = chewy muffins).
7. Fill muffin wells about 3/4 full.
8. Bake for 15-20 minutes or until edges are golden and toothpick comes out clean.

CUPCAKES

"They lie about marijuana. Tell you pot smoking makes you unmotivated. Lie! When you're high, you can do everything that you normally do, just as well. You just realize that it's not worth the fucking effort."

-Bill Hicks

Revolutionary Chocolate Cupcakes

Bring these cupcakes with you the next time you successfully infiltrate the Westborough Baptist Church or the Fed. Let's take this thing down from the inside of their stomachs.

Making cupcakes might not start a coup d'état, but doing something this wholesome with something that's so demonized, can help undermine the stigma surrounding a plant that helps people heal.

So, are we trying to change the world by putting cannabis in cute cupcakes and taking cute pictures of those cupcakes and saying cute things about the whole process? Yes, and it's going to be the most adorable revolution ever.

 2 Stoney Servings

OPTIONAL
Frost with Peanut Butter
Sriracha Frosting or
High Chai Frosting

INGREDIENTS

- ½ Cup GF Flour (Bob's)
- 1 t Baking Powder
- Pinch o' Salt
- ¼ Cup Sugar
- ¼ Cup High Quality Fair Trade Cocoa
- 2T Green Monsta Oil (Melted)
- Scant ¾ Cup Nut Milk
- ½ t Vanilla
- ¼ t Apple Cider Vinegar

METHOD

1. Preheat oven to 365°
2. Combine Flour, Baking Powder, Salt, Sugar and Cocoa Powder. Whisk!
3. Add wet ingredients and beat until all lumps/established regimes disappear.
4. Fill 4-5 cupcake liners 2/3 - 3/4 full.
5. Bake for 20 minutes or until toothpick comes out clean.
6. Allow to cool completely before frosting.

Thoughtless Cupcakes

The Buddhist philosophy of no thought awareness inspired these simple vanilla cupcakes. They're so simple that they require no input from your thinking machine. That thing could probably use some time off anyway.

Try to make these cupcakes while practicing no thought awareness. Every time a thought enters the space of your mind, simply acknowledge it, and let it pass. Then go back to feeling all of the sensations in your arm as it stirs the shit out of that batter, getting rid of all lumps, and clearing away all of the karma you brought with you from your past lives into your present-day kitchen.

You didn't think you were buying a meditation book, did you? Don't think. Just bake.

 2 Stoney Servings in 4-5 Cupcakes

OPTIONAL
Frost with High Chai Vanilla Frosting or Chocolate for Survival Frosting

INGREDIENTS

- ½ Cup GF Flour
  (Bob's Red Mill Blend is great for these)
- 1 t Baking Powder
- Pinch Salt
- ¼ Cup Sugar
- 2T Green Monsta Oil (melted)
- Scant ½ Cup of Nut Milk
- ½ t Vanilla
- ¼ t Apple Cider Vinegar

METHOD

1. Preheat oven to 365°
2. Combine Flour, Baking Powder, Salt and Sugar. Whisk!
3. Add wet ingredients and whisk until all lumps, visions of the future, and evaluations of the past disappear.
4. Fill 4-5 cupcake liners 2/3 full.
5. Bake for 20 minutes or until toothpick comes out clean.
6. Allow to cool completely before frosting.

Chili Chocolate Cupcakes

Looking for a cupcake with a kick!? These provide a one-two punch of dried chilis and cannabis.

It's better than a kick in the pants.

It's probably better than kickin' it with Kim Jong Un.

It's totally better than kicking rocks.

And it all happened because of Kickstarter.

Full circle!

🌿 2 Stoney Servings 🌿
2 Unfrosted Cupcakes = 1 Stoney Serving

INGREDIENTS

- ½ Cup GF Flour (Bob's Red Mill Blend)
- 1 t Baking Powder
- Pinch Salt
- 1/3 Cup Fair Trade Cocoa
- ½-1 t Hot Red Pepper Flakes
  (adjust to the level of heat your
  pepper flakes are packing)

- 2T Green Monsta Oil (melted)
- Scant ½ Cup of Nut Milk
- ½ t Vanilla
- ¼ t Apple Cider Vinegar
- ¼ Cup Sugar

METHOD

1. Preheat oven to 365°
2. Combine Flour, Baking Powder, Salt and Sugar. Whisk!
3. Add wet ingredients and whisk until completely smooth.
4. Fill 4-5 cupcake liners 2/3 full.
5. Bake for 20 minutes or until toothpick comes out clean.
6. Allow to cool completely before frosting.

OPTIONAL
Frost with Peanut
Butter Sriracha Frosting
or High Chai Frosting

COOKIES

Snickerdoodles

These were dubbed the "best weed food I've ever eaten" by one of our taste testers. After the words "vegan" and "gluten free" were tossed around, the same taste tester's mind was, "blown."

These Snickerdoodles are a wholesome Midwestern classic with a cannatwist. They're addicting as all get out, so be careful.

 4 Stoney Servings
2 Cookies = 1 Stoney Serving

INGREDIENTS

- ½ T Ground Flax + 2 T Water
- ¼ Cup Green Monsta Oil
- 1/3 Cup Pure Cane Sugar
- ½ t Vanilla
- 1 Cup GF Flour Blend (Bob's Red Mill)
- ¼ t Cream of Tartar
- ½ t Baking Soda
- Pinch of Cinnamon
- Cinnamon Sugar Coating:
  2 t Sugar + 2 t Cinnamon

METHOD

1. Combine Flax + Water. Set aside.
2. In a large bowl, cream Sugar, Green Monsta Oil and Vanilla until smooth.
3. Add Flax/Water Mix. Beat it!
4. In a separate bowl, combine GF Flour, Cream of Tartar, Baking Soda, and Cinnamon. Whisk!
5. Add the dry mix to the wet mix. Stir until just combined.
6. Roll dough into a ball, place in a covered container and refrigerate for an hour.
7. Preheat oven to 375°.
8. Remove dough from refrigerator. Roll into 8 equal sized balls.
9. Roll balls in Cinnamon Sugar Coating.
10 Bake for 10-12 minutes.

Merit Badge Cookies

The Merit Badge Cookie was inspired by the cookie-moving little girls who hang out outside of Jewel Osco. Those are some industrious little ladies.

And this is an industrious cookie undertaking. It's a three-part process that takes hours of baking and cooling time, quite a bit of prep, and caramel making. Yes. Caramel making. It's a scout-esque endeavor full of rich character-building experiences.

After making these, get to sewing your very own Marijuana Cooking merit badge. You've earned it.

 7-8 Stoney Servings
Makes about 8-10 Large Cookies

INGREDIENTS

MERT BADGE COOKIE
- ¼ Cup Green Monsta Oil (room temp)
- 2 T Sugar
- ¼ t Vanilla
- ½ T Nut Milk
- ½ Cup GF Flour
- Dash o' Baking Powder
- Dash o' Salt

CARAMEL COCONUT TOPPING
- 1/3 Cup Sugar
- ¼ Cup Shredded Coconut
- 1 ½ T Green Monsta Oil (melted)
- ¼ Cup Nut Milk (warmed)
- ¼ t Vanilla

CHOCOLATE DIP & DRIZZLE
- Ganashish (pg 84)

METHOD

MERIT BADGE COOKIE

1. Line baking sheet with parchment paper.
2. In a large mixing bowl, beat Green Monsta Oil, Sugar, Vanilla and Nut Milk.
3. In a separate bowl whisk GF Flour, Baking Powder and Salt.
4. Add Flour mix to Green Monsta mix. Knead the dough in the bowl.
5. Refrigerate dough for 20 minutes.
6. Preheat oven to 350°.
7. Roll out dough on a floured surface to 1/4 inch thickness.
8. Using a cookie cutter or a wide mouth glass, and a smaller cookie cutter or a water bottle cap, cut out cookies and place them on prepared baking sheet.
9. Bake about 10-12 minutes, until the edges get all golden.
10. Cool Completely before proceeding to the next step.

CARAMEL COCONUT TOPPING

1. In a clean, light colored pan, melt Sugar. Stir constantly.
2. After the Sugar begins to smoke and turn a rich reddish caramel color, carefully and quickly pour in Melted Green Monsta Oil and Warm Nut Milk. Whisk! Whisk more! Keep whisking! This part can be a huge dangerous mess. The melted sugar will react to the Oil & Nut Milk by sputtering, steaming and hissing. Stay alert. Stay vigilant. Then... whisk hard.
3. Take off heat. Add Coconut Flakes and Vanilla.
4. Spread onto cooled cookies. Refrigerate for 20-30 minutes.

CHOCOLATE DIP & DRIZZLE

1. Prepare Ganashish (page 84)

The Classic C3

There's nothing more classic or American than the Chocolate Chip Cookie. So get out the old star spangled banner, and get stoked that you live in a nation that believes in freedom... democracy... cookies!

And if you can't handle that, you should move to Canada. They hate cookies there.

 16 Stoney Servings

OPTIONAL
Add ¼ Cup Chopped Pecans or Walnuts

INGREDIENTS

- 2 ¼ Cup GF Flour
  (I used Pamela's Artisan Blend)
- 3/4 t Baking Soda
- 1 t Salt
- 1 Cup Green Monsta Oil
  (room temp)
- ¾ Cup Sugar
- ¾ Cup Brown Sugar
- 1 t Vanilla
- 2 Flaaxy Eggs
  (2 T Ground Flax + 6 T Water)
  or 2 Eggs
- 2 Cups Chocolate Chips

METHOD

1. Preheat oven to 350°.
2. Prepare a baking sheet by lightly greasing or using parchment paper.
3. In a large bowl, cream Green Monsta Oil, Sugars and Vanilla until smooth.
4. Add Flaaxy Eggs/Eggs. Beat it!
5. Slowly beat in Flour, Baking Soda and Salt.
6. Fold in Chocolate Chips.
7. Using a Tablespoon, scoop dough onto prepared baking sheet.
8. Bake 12-15 Minutes until edges are golden.
9. Remove from oven and allow to cool before serving.

Cookie Dough Bites

This is a sassy biotch remedy. If you or someone you love is confronted with overwhelming feelings of sassy, slap the following ingredients together in the way described below and experience a biotch recession. Back bitches, back! Here's some cookie dough.

These don't have any plans on going in the oven, but they will get you baked.

4 Stoney Servings

INGREDIENTS

- 1/4 Cup Green Monsta Oil (room temp)
- 1/4 Cup Brown Sugar
- 1/4 Cup Cane Sugar
- 1 t Vanilla Extract
- scant 1/4 Cup Nut Butter
- 1/2 Cup GF All Purpose Flour Mix
- 1 t Salt
- 1/2 Cup Chocolate Chips

SUBSTITUTION
Use conventional flour in place of the GF mix.

OPTIONAL
1/4 C Walnuts

1/4 C Dried Cherries

Drizzle with Ganashish (pg 84)

METHOD

1. Cream Green Monsta Oil, Brown Sugar & Cane Sugar with a fork until light and fluffy.
2. Add Nut Butter and Vanilla. Mix.
3. In separate bowl, whisk Flour and Salt together.
4. Combine bowls and mix.
5. Fold in Chocolate Chips.
6. Roll into balls, place on parchment paper lined plate or pan.

Thumbprint Cookies

Without them, thumb wars would be mighty boring. You couldn't hitchhike, pull up your pants or send a text message on a phone with a keypad (because those still exist).

Show some gratitude for your thumbs by sticking them in these delightful short-bread cookies. Then, stuff the imprint with peanut butter, jelly, chocolate kisses, etc. After that, eat those cookies and contemplate the evolutionary mutation that made the spacebar possible.

INGREDIENTS

- 1 ¼ Cups GF Flour
- Dash Salt
- 1/3 Cup Pure Cane Sugar
- 4 T Green Monsta Oil (melted)
- ½ t vanilla
- ¼ Cup Nut Milk (room temp)
- Peanut Butter and/or Jelly

 *3-4 Stoney Servings*

OPTIONAL
Try any type of jam or nut butter

METHOD

1. Preheat oven to 350° F. Line a pan or cookie sheet with parchment paper and put aside.

2. Combine flour, salt & sugar. Whisk!

3. Add melted Green Monsta Oil, vanilla and milk.

4. Mix and knead dough until smooth.

5. Pull 1" chunks off of the dough ball, and roll them into spheres.

6. Place cookies on parchment paper and press center with your thumb.

7. Fill thumb divot with Peanut Butter and Jelly.

8. Bake until golden (about 15-20 minutes).

No Bake Nut Butter Cookies

Riddle me this... Can one get baked without first baking? You bet your nut butter you can. These cookies are perfect for LOTR marathons. Don't want to miss Legolas hiking through the snowy mountains like the beautiful immortal weightless alabaster elf that he is? These cookies were designed for people like us.

 **2 Stoney Servings**

SUBSTITUTIONS
Choose any nut butter!
___
Dates =
1/4 C Raisins

OPTIONAL
Toast 1/8 C Sun-
flower Seeds w/ Salt
Add to processor
last for a chunkier,
saltier cookie.

INGREDIENTS

- 6 Dates
- 1/4 Cup Nut Butter *(I used an almond/PB blend)*
- 1/4 t Salt
- 1-2 T Green Monsta Oil
(These can get pretty oily if you use peanut butter. If you want to incorporate 2 T of green oil, use straight almond butter)

METHOD

1. Soak dates in 1 cup water for 1-2 hours.

2. Process all ingredients in food processor until smooth.

3. Roll into balls, place on parchment paper lined plate or pan.

4. Press with fork to make authentic fork decorated cookies.

5. Press with your finger if you don't want the other homeless appliance horders to think you're pretentious.

6. Refrigerate for 20 minutes.

Tahini Maple Sugar Cookies

Tahini? In a cookie? Okay. Let's start out by saying that you can sub out the tahini for any other finely ground nut butter. But if you've got some tahini on hand, just live a little. It's subtler than you'd expect, and it takes the edge off of a cookie that lives on the edge of being too sweet.

That being said, these cookies will undoubtedly satisfy your most rooted sweet tooth. They're a perfectly sweet accompaniment to apology notes, congratulatory notes, and practical notes that say:

"Cation: these cookies contain enough marjuana to anesthetize a small animal for several hours. Are you larger than a small animal? Help yourself!"

 4 Stoney Servings

INGREDIENTS

- 1 Cup All Purpose GF Flour
- ½ t Baking Powder
- ¼ t Salt
- ¼ Cup Tahini
- ¼ Cup Green Monsta Oil (room temp)
- ½ Cup Organic Pure Cane Sugar
- ½ t Vanilla
- ½ Cup Maple Syrup

METHOD

1. Preheat oven to 375°
2. Combine Flour, Baking Powder and Salt. Whisk!
3. Separately, combine Tahini, Green Monsta, Sugar, and Vanilla. Mash! Stir!
4. Slowly mix the dry mix into the wet mix.
5. Pour in Maple Syrup. Stir again!
6. Scoop 2 inch balls onto a parchment lined cookie sheet.
7. Press tops flat with a fork and sprinkle with Sugar.
8. Bake until lightly golden (about 15 minutes).

PIES & THINGS

"The illegality of cannabis is outrageous, an impediment to full utilization of a drug which helps produce the serenity and insight, sensitivity and fellowship so desperately needed in this increasingly mad and dangerous world."

- Carl Sagan

Apple Crisp

The apple tree is thought to be the first ever cultivated by humans. It calls to mind a lot of firsts. Like:

> The first time you smoked marijuana.
> The first time you baked with it.
> The first time you ate that thing you baked with it.
> The first time you put marijuana in an apple crisp, baked it, ate it, and couldn't remember if you already ate it and ate more of it.

Oh, sweet firsts. This is a simple apple crisp with a ganja twist, so if this is your first edible or your first apple crisp, it's a perfect place to start.

 4 Stoney Servings

INGREDIENTS

- 6 Apples
  (Sliced 1/4 inch thick)
- 2-3 T Sugar
- ¾ t Cinnamon
- ¼ t Salt
- ½ Cup Brown Sugar
- ½ Cup Rolled Oats
- 1/3 Cup GF Flour
- 4 T Green Monsta Oil
  (cold & cut into small chunks)

METHOD

1. Preheat oven to 350°.
2. Grease 8x8 pan.
3. Coat Apple Slices with Sugar, Cinnamon & Salt Mix.
4. Pour Coated Apples into prepped Pan.
5. Mix Brown Sugar, Oats and Flour.
6. Using your fingers, incorporate cold chunks of Green Monsta Oil.
7. Bake about an hour, until topping is crispy and apples are soft. Serve warm.

Ripped Rice Crispy Pie

This is proof that anything is sweeter when turned into a pie. Pie shaped things always seem to vanish faster too. This thing made such a fast disappearing act that Chris Angel called it to do a Spike TV special in Las Vegas. Zing!

We used a bag of these awesome vegan marshmallows called Dandies, but you can use half of a bag of conventional minis if that's what's available in your area.

🌿 *4 Stoney Servings* 🌿

INGREDIENTS

- ¼ Cup Green Monsta Oil
- 1 Bag (10 oz) Dandies Vegan Marshmallows (Quartered) or ½ of a 16 oz Bag of Mini Marshmallows
- 1 t Vanilla
- 1 t Cinnamon
- 3-3 ½ Cups Puffed Rice
  (*Organic puffed rice is longer and denser than conventional rice crispies. Use less if using organic puffed rice.*)

OPTIONAL
Drizzle with Ganashish and place back into the fridge for 10-15 minutes
———
Add 2 T Green Monsta Oil to turn this into a six person pie

METHOD

1. Melt Green Monsta Oil over low heat.
2. Once melted, begin stirring in marshmallows a little at a time
3. Add Vanilla and Cinnamon and stir until all marshmallows have melted into a ball of green goo.
4. Add Puffed Rice one cup at a time until your mixture is still sticky, but pliable.
5. Remove from heat and immediately press into a greased pie dish.
6. Set it lovingly in the fridge for about 20 minutes.
7. Cut into slices and serve.

Ethel's Sweede Pie

If you've already read the Roasted Veggie Quiche Meditation, you know that crusts aren't always a way to a stress free, zenned out, lifestyle. Ethel's Sweede Pie flips that upside down. The crust goes on top, instantly turning your kitchen into an "f" word free environment. Isn't that the best "f"wording news you've heard all day!?

When my college bestie, Ethel, sent over this recipe, it had almost two sticks of butter in it. We cleaned out our filthy cussing mouths, and then cleaned all of the butter out of this pie. However, if you're a butter user, I can't imagine a better way to work your way towards your very first bypass.

This recipe is dedicated to Ethel and her Sweetie Cannon. May they have many years of buttery bliss together.

INGREDIENTS

Filling:
- 1-2 Apples
- 1 T Sugar
- 1 t Cinnamon

Topping:
- ¾ Cup Green Monsta Oil (soft)
- 1 Cup Pure Cane Sugar
- 1 Egg or 1 Flaaxy Egg
- 1 Cup Flour
- ¼ Cup Pecans (optional)
- ¼ t Salt

 12 Stoney Servings

OPTIONAL
Add ½ t Nutmeg
¼ t Ginger,
¼ t Allspice
into the filling

METHOD

1. Preheat oven to 350°.

2. Heavily grease a pie tin.

3. Create two layers of thinly sliced apples in the bottom of the pan.

4. Sprinkle Sugar and Cinnamon over the apples.

5. Mix all topping ingredients together until it becomes a paste.

6. Spread on top of apples.

7. Bake for 45 minutes.

MothaLovin' Pumpkin Pie

Do you have an extensive vocabulary of explicit words? If so, I'd like you to know that you can step away from the bar of soap. Swearing and using "offensive" words reportedly increases circulation, alleviates pain, elevates endorphins, and leads to an overall sense of well-being. Isn't that shit amazing?!

Just don't cuss around your mother, because your mother probably doesn't know about the endorphins and circulation, and she probably won't care how good dropping f-bombs is for your mental and physical health. Dammit.

I made this pie crust using spelt and gluten free flour, and while it made for a rustic and delicious pie (and a fairly easy crust to work with), it is not gluten free. Feel free to sub more GF flour for the spelt. Or use a premade GF pie crust.

INGREDIENTS

THE CRUST
1 Cup Spelt Flour
1 Cup GF Flour
¼ Cup Sugar
2 T Ground Flax
1 t Cinnamon
¼ t Kosher Salt
½ Cup Almond Milk
½ Cup Green Monsta Oil (melted)

THE FILLING
2 ¼ Cup Canned Pumpkin
½ Cup Brown Sugar
¼ Cup Full Fat Coconut Milk
1 T Coconut Oil (room temp)
¼ Cup Maple Syrup
3 t Cornstarch or Tapioca Starch
2 t Vanilla
2 t Cinnamon
½ t Ground Ginger
½ t Nutmeg

☘ 8 Stoney Servings ☘

METHOD

THE CRUST
1. Preheat oven to 425°.
2. In a large bowl, mix dry crust ingredients (Flours, Sugar, Flax, Cinnamon and Salt).
3. Add Nut Milk and melted Green Monsta Oil. Mix just until the dough forms into a few lumps.
4. Turn dough out onto a floured surface. Roll out dough until it's a few inches wider than your pie dish.
5. Gently roll the dough onto rolling pin and unroll it over your pie dish.
6. Tuck the edges of the dough under and make the crust look perdy by crimping the edges. Poke a few fork holes in the bottom and bake for 7 minutes.
7. Roll out any extra dough and cut it into thematic shapes.

THE FILLING
1. Whisk together Maple and Tapioca/Cornstarch.
2. Add remaining filling ingredients. Whisk!

THE PIE
1. Preheat oven to 350°.
2. Scoop filling into crust and smooth. Place thematically shaped cut outs on the top.
3. Bake for 45 minutes. Remove and cover crust edges with tinfoil (optional). Bake for another 15 minutes. Cool for an hour.
4. Transfter to fridge to set for several hours or overnight.

SWEET MUNCHIES

Fudge Nuggets

Is it fudge? Arguably, but people seem to get really amused when you call it fudge. They look at you pitifully and think, "Awww.... this little health nut thinks this is what fudge is... Isn't that cute?" It's just too damn healthy to be fudge. So just go with it, and when you get another pitiful glance from someone standing by your fudge tray, you can turn up the volume and share your cholesterol numbers with the unexpecting partygoer next to you. Because you, are the life of the party.

This recipe is super simple, and can be tossed together in about five minutes. Stick it in the freezer and it's ready to go out the door with you in ten.

INGREDIENTS

- 1/2 Cup Green Monsta Oil
- 1/2 Cup Almond Butter
- 1/8 to 1/4 Cup Honey
- 1/2 of a Banana, Mashed
- 1 tsp Vanilla Extract

 8 Stoney Servings

OPTIONAL
Use any kind of nut butter

Add 1/8 Cup Dried Fruit

Add 1/8 Cup Chocolate Chips

METHOD

Option 1: Place all ingredients in small pot over low heat until things begin to melt, around 30 seconds. Blend with an immersion blender until smooth.

Option 2: Place all ingredients in a food processor or blender. Blend for several minutes until smooth.

2. Pour into a loaf pan lined with parchement paper. For larger chunks, use a mini loaf pan or double the recipe.

3. Refrigerate or freeze until firm.

4. Cut into 8 equal squares.

Special Brownie Bites

You're special. You're like a unique snowflake with an intricate pattern, a distinct dance. You special little snowflake, you.

No one has the same genetic material that codes every cell in your body. There has truly never been anyone like you, and there never will be.

Even your very own DNA expresses itself differently throughout your life. If you learn a new skill or eat too much sugar (wink wink), one marker can switch off or another can switch on, so the evolutionary process that is constantly occurring within you can support the decisions you make, helping you become who you want to be on a physical and chemical level.

This means that even on a cellular level, you're newly special every moment of the day. The you that is reading this book right now is literally not the same person who picked it up. Isn't it amazing?

No. It's science. And science says your special. These brownie bites are special too... Because they have weed in them.

 8 Stoney Servings
1 Brownie Bite = 1 Serving

OPTIONAL
Add 1/3 Cup Walnuts or Mini Chocolate Chips
———
Frost with Sriracha Peanut Butter Frosting

INGREDIENTS

- ¾ Cup Pure Cane Sugar
- ¾ T Baking Powder
- ¼ t Salt
- ½ Cup Fair Trade Cocoa
- ½ Cup Green Monsta Oil (Melted)
- 2 T Flax + 6 T Water (or 2 Eggs)
- 1 T Vanilla
- ¾ Cup GF Flour (Bob's)

METHOD

1. Preheat oven to 350° & grease 8 wells of a standard muffin tin.

2. In a small bowl, mix Flax with Water. Let Flaaxy Eggs sit for 5 minutes.

3. Whisk Sugar, Baking Powder, Salt, and Cocoa in a large bowl.

4. Add Green Monsta Oil, Flaaxy Eggs (or Eggs), and vanilla. Stir!

5. Fold in GF flour ¼ cup at a time.

6. Fold in optional ingredients (Walnuts or Mini Chocolate Chips).

7. Scoop the thick batter into the greased muffin wells (3/4 full).

8. Bake for 18-24 minutes.

9. Here's the kicker: pull them out as soon as they begin to pull away from the sides of the tin and when they spring back when lightly poked.

10 Allow to cool.

Note: Don't forget to label any of your "special" baked goods if you plan on storing them for any amount of time.

Sweet Tater Fry Bread

Don't you just love it when a fail turns into a win? This fry bread recipe started as a biscuit recipe that was way too chewy. I'm talking about a Star Wars supporting character gargling with Quaker granola bars kind of chewy. Wakka wakka!

Make this sweet fry bread flatter than you'd think. It puffs up quite a bit and will have a gooey center if it's too thick when it hits the frying pan.

It's almost sweet enough to pretend it's a doughnut. If you want to go the purely sweet route, serve with jam or fresh preserves. If you're looking for something sweet and savory, serve with fried eggs and salsa or sliced avocado with salt and Sriracha (vegan).

 4 Stoney Servings

INGREDIENTS

- 1/2 Cup Mashed Sweet Tater
- ¼ Cup Monsta Oil (room temp)
- 1/4 Cup of Water
- Extra Water as Needed (1/4- ½ Cup)
- 1/2 T Baking Powder

- 1 T Apple Cider Vinegar
- 1/4 Cup Maple Syrup/Agave
- ¾-1 ½ Cups GF Flour
- High Temp Oil (grapeseed) for frying

METHOD

1. Combine Mashed Sweet Tater and Monsta Oil. Mash.
2. Add Maple Syrup/Agave. Mix.
3. Add Apple Cider Vinegar and Baking Powder. Fold.
4. Stir in ½ Cup Flour at a time. Add Water as needed.
5. Fold in Flour and Water until dough is fluffy and barely dry enough to press out by hand.
6. Lightly knead dough in bowl.
7. Pour High Temp Oil into a high walled pan over medium-high heat.
8. Test the oil temp by placing dough nuggets into it. Oil is ready when nuggets quickly turn golden and are cooked all the way through.
9. Tear off a hunk of dough and flatten to about a ¼ inch thickness. Fry.
10. Adjust dough thickness and heat as necessary.
12. Place on a paper towel to cool and drain off excess grease.

SALTY MUNCHIES

"*In strict medical terms, marijuana is far safer than many foods we commonly consume. For example, eating 10 raw potatoes can result in a toxic response. By comparison, it is physically impossible to eat enough marijuana to induce death. Marijuana in its natural form is one of the safest therapeutically active substances known to man. By any measure of rational analysis marijuana can be safely used within the supervised routine of medical care.*"

[DEA Administrative Law Judge - 1988]
- Francis Young

Potcorn

Fact #1: Popcorn is not a breakfast.

Fact #2: Popcorn is not a baked good.

Fact #3: Potcorn is a house favorite at Wake & Bake HQ.

Fact #4: Theme be damned. It's goin' in the book.

Fact #5: Archeologists found 1,000+ year old popcorn that still looks white and fluffy when they blew the dust off.

Fact #6: Potcorn would never last that long.

INGREDIENTS

- 1t High Temp Oil (Grapeseed)
- ¼ Cup Potcorn
- 1 T Melted Green Monsta Oil (per person)
- Salt, Pepper, Nut Yeast, Other Herbs (to taste)

🌿 *1-4 Stoney Servings* 🌿

METHOD

1. Put a large pot over med-high heat.
2. Once pot is hot, add High Temp Oil (Grapeseed) and three unpopped kernels. Cover.
3. When the three kernels pop, remove the pot and pour in the rest of the popcorn.
4. Cover and shake the pot to coat the kernels in oil. Count to 30.
5. Place pot back on the heat.
6. This method allows you to homogenize the temperature of the kernels, making them pop at relatively the same time. You shouldn't have much unpopped popcorn in the bottom of your pot.
7. Pour into separate bowls and drizzle 1 T Melted Green Monsta Oil on each bowl.
8. Sprinkle with Salt, Pepper, Nutritional Yeast, or Other Herbs. Serve warm.

Herb -N- Herb Nut Cheese

This ganja infused nut cheeze is dairy free, protein-y and savory as all get out. Spread it on bagels. Pour it on breakfast tacos. Dip your cracker ass crackers or tortilla chips up in there.

🌿 *1/2 cup = 1 stoney serving* 🌿

Ingredients

- 1 Cup Soaked Sunflower Seeds
- 1 Cup Soaked Almonds
- 2 Cups H20 + Extra
- 1/4 Cup Ganja Oil
- 1.5 Cups Basil/Cilantro
- Salt to Taste

OPTIONAL
1-3 TBSP Favorite Hot Sauce
___
Nutritional Yeast to Taste

ALTERNATIVES
Add more water for more of a "saucy" cheeze
___
Try other soaked nuts and seeds

Method

1. Soak almonds & sunflower seeds overnight. Discard soaking water.

2. Combine all ingredients in food processor.

3. Process until creamy.

Pothead Pesto

Morgan Freeman once called cannabis "God's own weed."

The man who appears in movies to recap every plotline, who remembers every detail you forgot, who puts it all together in a meaningful and succinct monologue, is (or was at one time) a pothead.

So why aren't we over the stigma yet? The word pothead is considered by some to have negative connotations, and some argue that it's only used as a derogatory term. But, as a wise man once said, "to be offended by a word is to give it power." Morgan Freeman probably said that.

Let's take the word "Pothead" back. And let's put it into pesto for safekeeping.

🌿 **4 Stoney Servings** 🌿
Approx ¼ Cup = 1 Stoney Serving

INGREDIENTS

- 2 Cups of a Leafy Herb: Basil, Cilantro, or Parsley (stemmed)
- ½ Cup Sunflower Seeds (toasted) or Pine Nuts
- 1 Cloves Garlic
- ¼ Green Monsta Oil (Melted)
- Salt

METHOD

1. Toast Sunflower Seeds over medium heat until aromatic and golden. Cool.
2. Combine Leafy Herb, Sunflower Seeds and Garlic in a food processor. Pulse until coarse.
3. Slowly add Monsta Oil in a drizzle while pulsing the processor. Process until it becomes a smooth paste.
4. Season with Salt to taste.

I met the farmer at Colorado's oldest organic farm and intentional community. There, we learned a lot about growing food, community dynamics, farming, love, patience. and mostly... we learned about hippies.

These shakes were inspired by our time among the hippies at the Buff. They were sweet and special times. These are sweet and special shakes. Same, same, but different.

HIPPIE SHAKES

The Trust Fund Hippie Shake

Let me begin by saying there's nothing wrong with trust fund hippies (ie trustifarians). They're just doing their thing. Their thing just happens to be living in destitution, while they float on the lazy river of an inherited trust fund. To each his own.

Did you know that Marie Antoinette built her own peasant village at Versailles and used to play commoner on the weekend? It's hard being queen. It's also hard being one of the trustifari.

Like Marie on the weekends, and trust fund hippies living in communes, this shake has a lot of hidden dough.

Sure, it's richer, but that doesn't make it better than all of the other shakes.

 **1 Stoney Servings**

Ingredients

- 1 Scoop Ice Cream
  (Coconut Dream Vanilla)

- ½ Cup Nut Milk

- 2 T Stooonie Crisp Cookie Dough
  (or any other type of cookie dough)

- 1 T Melted Green Monsta Oil

Method

1. Blend Ice Cream, Nut Milk and Cookie Dough.

2. While blending, drizzle melted coconut oil into the blender.

3. Serve immediately (oil will solidify eventually)

The Dirty Hippie Shake

The slyest and most magical hippie living in a commune is the dirty hippie. The dirty hippie has the power to leave crusty dishes around the communal kitchen without being detected. He or she can shave off all of his or her body hair and leave it in the bathroom sink for weeks without anyone being able to confront the clean-shaven offender. That's some filthy magic.

The Akaname, a Japanese mythical creature, is said to come into your bathroom at night and lick it clean. A message to the dirty hippie: The Akaname doesn't exist. Just clean the bathroom.

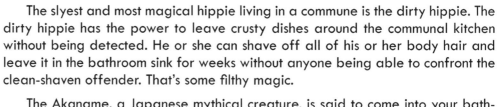

🌿 *1 Stoney Servings* 🌿

INGREDIENTS

- 1 Scoop Ice Cream
  (Coconut Dream Vanilla)
- ½ Cup Nut Milk
- 2-3 T Cookie Crumbles
  (Leftover Stoooooonie Crisp or
  any other GF/Vegan Cookie)
- ½-2 t Cocoa Powder
- 1 T Melted Green Monsta Oil

METHOD

1. Blend Ice Cream, Nut Milk, Cookie Crumbles and Cocoa Powder.
2. While blending, drizzle melted coconut oil into the blender.
3. Serve immediately (oil will solidify eventually)

The Doc Bronner Hippie Shake

What hippie doesn't love Dr. Bronner's soap? But do we really know much about the man whose soaps have kept commune members armpits periodically clean, and whose bottles have made for the most bizarrely entertaining bathroom reading?

Emanual H. Bronner's was born to the Heilbronner family of soap makers in Germany. In 1929, he emigrated to the US fearing that the Nazi party would take power and that his Jewish family would be persecuted. His mother and father refused to leave the country. Years later, in a censored postcard, his father wrote, "You were right. —Your loving father." That was the last time he heard from either of his parents.

But... How did he still have so much faith in humanity? Why wasn't he cynical or bitter? We'll probably never know where the moral fortitude of Doc Bronner originates. Just drink these minty shakes, and cleanse yourself of the most depressing factoid in this cookbook.

INGREDIENTS

- 1 Scoop Ice Cream
  (Coconut Dream Vanilla)

- ½ Cup Nut Milk

- 1-2 T Fresh Mint (diced) or
  ½-1 t peppermint extract

- 1 T Melted Green Monsta Oil

 1 Stoney Servings

METHOD

1. Blend Ice Cream, Nut Milk and Mint.

2. While blending, drizzle melted coconut oil into the blender.

3. Serve immediately (oil will solidify eventually).

DRANKS & COFFEE CREAMERS

Green Drank

This is far and away the healthiest recipe in Wake & Bake: a cookbook. It's the only thing within these pages that you could probably eat every day without getting a mouth full of cavities and "Advanced Glycation End Products". Who knew that cookies would make you age faster? Scientists. They totally called it.

It's an apple, some kale, lemon juice, and maybe some spirulina... But just because it's simple and good, doesn't mean it ain't gangsta. Introducing: Green Drank.

🌿 *1 Stoney Serving* 🌿

INGREDIENTS

- 2 Large Leaves of Kale
  (I used Lasanato/Dino Kale)

- 1 Apple

- 1 t Apple Cider Vinegar/Lemon Juice

- 1 t Spirulina
  (optional, but recommended)

- 1.5-2 Cups Water

- 1 T Green Monsta Oil (melted)

METHOD

1. Blend all ingredients except the Green Monsta Oil.

2. When blended, and with the blender running, drizzle in Green Monsta Oil.

3. Serve immediately. Oil will eventually solidify.

75

Highly Evolved Creamer

This creamer is vegan, sugar free, glutenfree, dairyfree, non-gmo, and organic. It's simple, pure and it won't spike your blood sugar. It will, however, get your adrenals pumping if you put it into regular coffee.

It will help you either reach enlightenment before 9am, or it will have you filling out three reams of paperwork to get your firstborn child into an extremely competitive Montessori kindergarten spot.

But you don't even have a first born, yet.

That's crazy ambition.

Pour it in your coffee sparingly if you have things to accomplish during the day. Use the entire recipe if you feel that accomplishment is an illusion.

INGREDIENTS

- 3-4 T Coconut Milk
- 1 T Melted Green Monsta Oil
- 1 t Nut Milk

 1 Stoney Serving

METHOD

1. Blend! Use in hot coffee. If it becomes cold, the oil will separate.

Hippie Speedball Creamer

The Hippie Speedball is a classic wake and bake move. It's a simple pairing of coffee and a joint in the morning.

The joint gets you ready to face the day. The coffee allows you to stay awake for it, so you can excitedly ramble on about what a weird word "shallow" is.

Seriously... say it... and think it... now say it again... weird, right?

This recipe works best in a high-speed blender. I used an attachment that came with a hand blender I got at a thrift store for three bucks. If you don't have anything that will work, skip back to the Highly Evolved Creamer for a less needy coffee creamer recipe.

 3-4 Stoney Servings

About 1 Half Cup = 1 Stoney Serving

Ingredients

- 8 Dates Soaked in ½ Cup Boiling Water
- 1 ½ Cups Unsweetened Nut Milk
- ½ T Vanilla
- Pinch Salt
- 3 T Monsta Oil (melted)
- 2 T Tapioca Flour + 1 ½ T Cold Water

Method

1. Pour Boiling Water over Dates. Soak for at least 15 minutes.
2. Mix Tapioca flour and Cold Water in small bowl. Set aside.
3. Blend Dates and their Soaking Water until completely combined.
4. Add Nutmilk, Vanilla, and Salt. Pulse.
5. Add Melted Monsta Oil. Pulse.
6. Add Tapioca Flour mix. Pulse.
7. Store in a glass jar. Creamer will get a bit thicker as it cools.

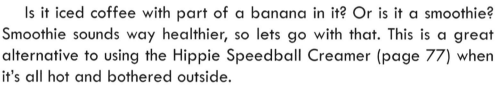

Hippie Speedball Smoothie

Is it iced coffee with part of a banana in it? Or is it a smoothie? Smoothie sounds way healthier, so lets go with that. This is a great alternative to using the Hippie Speedball Creamer (page 77) when it's all hot and bothered outside.

  *1 Stoney Serving*

INGREDIENTS

- 1.5 Cups Cold Coffee
- 1/3 Cup Nut Milk
- ½ Cup Canned Coconut Milk
- ½-1 Banana (Frozen, Chilled or Room Temp)
- 1-3 t Honey or Agave
- 1 T Green Monsta Oil (Melted)
- 1 t Cinnamon (optional)

METHOD

1. Add Coffee, Nut Milk, Coconut Milk, Banana, Agave/Honey, and Cinnamon into a blender. Blend!
2. While the blender is rolling, drizzle in Melted Green Monsta oil.
3. Sprinkle with Cinnamon.
4. Drink asap. Oil will eventually separate.

FROSTINGS & STUFF

"Federal and state laws (should) be changed to no longer make it a crime to possess marijuana for private use."

- Richard M. Nixon

High Chai Frosting

This frosting is excellent on Pot Tarts, Cupcakes and Special Brownie Bites. The longer you steep your tea bag (loose chai in a tea ball works too), the more your frosting will taste like an exotic Indian adventure. The more powdered sugar you put in it, the more it will taste like a tub of store bought frosting. The choice is yours.

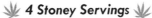 *4 Stoney Servings*

INGREDIENTS

- ¼ Cup Green Monsta Oil
- 1.5-2 Cups Powdered Sugar
- 1 Bag Chai Tea
- 1 T Boiling Water
- 1 T Nut Milk
- 1 t Cinnamon

OPTIONAL
Add ¼- ½ t Tapioca Starch or GF Flour to thicken for piping and decorating

METHOD

1. Brew Chai Tea to extra strength in 1 T Boiling Water. Let steep for 10 minutes.

2. Using a food processor, pulse Green Monsta Oil until smooth.

3. Add Nut Milk. Pulse.

4. Add Chai Tea Concentrate, Powdered Sugar, and Cinnamon. Pulse until smooth.

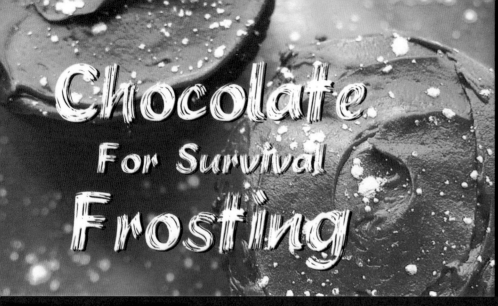

Chocolate
For Survival
Frosting

After spending weeks in the Kalalau River Valley, the farmer and I were finally headed back to civilization. We hadn't had cell phones, the internet, or coffee in almost a month.

We were only a mile from the end of the eleven mile trail when we were stopped by a man wearing two different shoes, carrying a small plastic bag and holding a large walking stick. He asked us a few questions about the state of the valley and seemed pleased with our report. When we asked him how long he was planning on staying, he reached into his bag and pulled out a half-eaten bag of cacao nibs. "As long as these will let me."

He went on to describe his beliefs about the impact cacao had on sustaining the human body. It was a superfood, he said. And he planned on eating and trading this superfood to stay in the jungle for as long as possible. I often think of this man and his plan to live off of raw chocolate (i.e. cacao) for as long as possible. He is a Hero.

If you'd like to turn a superfood into a frosting, throw a bunch of sugar at it and blend it. Huzzah! You'll live forever.

INGREDIENTS

- ¼ Cup Green Monsta Oil

- 1.5-2 Cups Powdered Sugar

- 3-6 T Nut Milk

- 1/3 Cup High Quality Cocoa Powder

 4 Stoney Servings

METHOD

1. Put Green Monsta oil into a food processor. Beat it.

2. Add 3 T Nut Milk. Beat it.

3. Add the rest of the ingredients. Because no one likes to be defeated.

4. Process until smooth. For a smoother frosting, use more Nut Milk. For decorating, use less.

82

Peanut Butter
Sriracha Frosting

The farmer and I were stranded in the Mojave dessert. Our 1979 Subaru Brat broke down in Baker, CA, home of the largest thermometer in the world and nothing else. The mechanic said we needed a rare part, and they spent four days looking for it while we camped in the dessert and waited for news.

We were broke and had nothing on us but some cans of soup, a loaf of bread, a tub of peanut butter and a bottle of Sriracha.

We loaded peanut butter on spoons and squirted Sriracha on it for breakfast. We smeared it on campfire toast for lunch. This was clearly the beginning of the rest of our lives. Even though we never found the part (and the Brat didn't get fixed until 3 months later) we obliviously spent our short time in the desert dreaming about a future filled with this perfect condiment combination.

Welcome to the future.

 4 Stoney Servings

INGREDIENTS

- ½ Cup Creamy Peanut Butter
- ¼ Cup Green Monsta Oil (room temp)
- 1 Cup Powdered Sugar
- 1.5 T Nut Milk

METHOD

1. Blend all ingredients in a food processor or blender until smooth.

2. Pipe or spread on everything.

Ganashish

It's everything that melted chocolate should be: sweet, easy, and filled with cannabis. It contains about 1-2 stoney servings with each batch, so it's a nice way to add a little ummmph to other Wake & Bake goodies. You can also use it for a great drizzle or a dipping sauce for non W&B items. Leave out the Green Monsta Oil for a pure chocolate experience.

1-2 Stoney Servings

INGREDIENTS

- ¼-1/2 Cup Chocolate Chips
- 1-2 T Green Oil
- 1 1/2 Cups Water
  *(to be used for melting...
  do not add to the chocolate)*

METHOD

1. Fill small pot or double boiler with 1 ½ cups water.
2. Bring water to a boil.
3. If using a small pot, find a metal mixing bowl that will fit snuggly on top.
4. Pour chocolate chips and oil into the metal mixing bowl or top of the double boiler.
5. If using small pot, place bowl on the pot.
6. Stir! Until completely melted.
7. Use immediately. Drizzle it on anything. Dip anything in it.
8. If chocolate hardens, reheat using the same method.

Vavavanilla Icing

This is a magically simple icing recipe that will add some buzz to non Wake & Bake goodies. You can use it to add stoney servings to other recipes in this book as well. It can also be made with regular coconut oil, so you can get to work on time, and you'll actually arrive at the right building. You have options.

 4 Stoney Servings

INGREDIENTS

- 2 Cups Powdered Sugar

- ¼ Cup Green Monsta Oil

- 2 T Nut Milk/Coconut Milk

- 1 Dash Salt

METHOD

1. Combine all ingredients in food processor or blender.

2. Before use, head in a double boiler or in the microwave until smooth and drizzly.

CHOCOLATES

Choose Your Own Adventure Chocolates

You're right in the middle of reading a cannabis cookbook. To your left, recipes. To your right, more recipes. Below, you see one for chocolates. There are three delicious options that you could possibly make. You know that it would only take a matter of minutes and you could pull delicious infused chocolates out of your freezer. If you want to do this, read the instructions below. If not, turn to page 34.

 8 Stoney Servings

INGREDIENTS

- ½ Cup Green Monsta Oil
- ¼ Cup Cocoa Powder
- 2-4 T Liquid Sweetner (to taste) (Agave, Maple Syrup or Honey)
- 1 t Vanilla
- ½ t Salt
- FOR SEEDY: ¼ Cup Sunflower Seeds
- FOR MINT: 2-4 T Chopped Fresh Mint
- FOR COCONUT: 4-6 T Toasted Coconut Flakes

METHOD

1. FOR SEEDY or COCONUT: Place Sunflower Seeds or Coconut Flakes in a small pan over med-high heat. Add Salt and stir occasionally until seeds are aromatic and golden-red. Allow to cool.
2. In a double boiler (or metal mixing bowl fitted atop a pot), melt Green Monsta Oil and Liquid Sweetner.
3. Add Cocoa Powder. Whisk!
4. Remove from heat and fold in toasted Sunflower Seeds.
5. Pour into a muffin tin, cupcake liners, or mini cupcake liners.
6. Freeze for 10-15 minutes before serving.
7. Store in refrigerator or freezer.

Seedy Truffles

Truffles are traditionally the sweetest and fanciest of all the candies. So use the word truffle and let everyone think you're refined… even if you're more of a seedy, back alley kind of character.

But how do you know if you're a seedy character? Take the quiz below. Don't worry. There are no wrong answers.

INGREDIENTS

- ½ Cup Coconut Flakes
- 1 Cup Sunflower Seeds
- 6 T Cocoa Powder
- ¼ Cup Liquid Sweetner (Maple, Agave, Honey)
- ¼ Cup Green Monsta Oil (room temp)
- 1 t Salt
- 1 T Vanilla
- 1-2 Batches of Ganashish (page 84. Optional but Recommended)

4 Stoney Servings

a. Has anyone ever described you as burly, extremely bearded, or gruff?
b. Do you like hiding in the shadows or behind refuse?
c. Is your favorite phrase, "Give me everything you've got and I won't have to use this shiv" or "I made these knuckledusters out of some bale wire and duct tape?"

If you answered yes to any of the above, you might be a seedy character. To cope, make these seedy truffles, shave, and find a hobby that doesn't include makeshift weaponry.

OPTIONAL
Toast Sunflower Seeds and Coconut Flakes for a warmer and more complex flavor

SUBSTITUTION
Walnuts instead of Sunflower Seeds

METHOD

1. Blend Coconut Flakes and Sunflower Seeds for about 30 seconds.
2. Add all remaining ingredients.
3. Press into a glass container or small baking dish.
4. Refrigerate for 20 minutes.
5. Remove from fridge and roll into balls. Place on parchment lined baking sheet.
6. Freeze for 20 minutes.
7. Dip and Drizzle with Ganashish.

PB Cups

freshly ground organic roasted peanut butter + chocolate + cannabis = omfgasdfakljlp (translation: they are very very good)

INGREDIENTS
- ½ Cup Green Monsta Oil
- ¼ Cup Cocoa Powder
- 2 T Liquid Sweetner
  (Agave, Maple Syrup or Honey)
- 1 t Vanilla
- 2-4 T Creamy Peanut Butter

  8 Stoney Servings

METHOD

1. In a double boiler (or metal mixing bowl fitted atop a pot), melt Green Monsta Oil and Liquid Sweetner.
2. Add Cocoa Powder. Whisk!
3. Remove from heat.
4. Pour half of the Liquid Chocolate Mix in a muffin tin, cupcake liners, or mini cupcake liners.
5. Freeze for 10-15 minutes.
6. Remove from freezer and scoop Peanut Butter into the center of each cup. Flatten the peanut butter a bit, leaving the edges available to make the chocolate seal.
7. Pour Liquid Chocolate Mix to cover the peanut butter.
8. Freeze for another 10-15 minutes before serving.
9. Store in refrigerator or freezer.

Not Normal Chocolates

These chocolates aren't normal. They're simple, easy and fast, but they're definitely not normal. Feel free to add more of your chosen sweetener to make them sweeter or more cocoa to give them more chocolate intensity.

INGREDIENTS

- ½ Cup Green Monsta Oil
- ¼ Cup Cocoa Powder
- 2 T Liquid Sweetner
  (Agave, Maple Syrup or Honey)
- 1 t Vanilla

 **8 Stoney Servings**

METHOD

1. In a double boiler (or metal mixing bowl fitted atop a pot), melt Green Monsta Oil and Liquid Sweetner.
2. Add Cocoa Powder. Whisk
3. Pour into a muffin tin, cupcake liners, or mini cupcake liners.
4. Freeze for 10-15 minutes before serving.
5. Store in refrigerator or freezer.

THE END

CONVERSION CHART

GREEN MONSTA OIL	1 Cup	1 Cup Ganja Butter
BAKING POWDER	1 teaspoon	1/4 t baking soda + 1/2 t lemon juice
COCONUT MILK	1 Cup	1 Cup Whole Milk
FLAAXY EGG	1 T Ground Flax + 3 T Water	1 Egg
NUT MILK	1 Cup	1 Cup 1% Milk
BROWN SUGAR	1 Cup firmly packed	1 cup granulated sugar + 1/4 cup unsulphered molasses
HONEY, AGAVE, MAPLE	1 Cup	1 1/4 cup granulated sugar + 1/4 cup liquid called for in recipe
GF FLOUR	1 Cup	1 Cup Wheat Flour (in most cases)

THANK YOU

Without the time and space provided at Elsewhere Studios in the beautifully bizarre Paonia, CO, this book wouldn't have even been a puff of imagination. Thank you so much Karen, Willow and Maya for everything you've done with that space and for creating the artist in residence program. You all make dreams come to life.

Aja, I love you. You came in at the 11th hour and your perseverance, talent and hard work are the only reason this book got finished this year. It's been an honor working with you and seeing your confidence grow as we created this together. You're such a beautiful woman, and even though we've known each other since we were children, I've been very lucky to get to know you again as an adult. Oh... and this book is a placenta. Thanks for touching it lovingly.

Nate, I noticed that you made almost every non-cookbook meal since September. That was awesome. Thank you for not allowing me to take anything too seriously, but still knowing how much finishing this meant to me. I'm a very lucky woman to be able to walk through this life with you. I love you.

Ayana, you are a goddess. Without your loving support when my confidence wavered, this ground up tree that you're holding would have never been put to use as this cookbook. Thank you for helping a tree reach the pinnacle of its evolution (and for being the inspiringly beautiful, open and authentic woman that you are).

Mom, Sally, Evan, Lando, Eric, and Brandy, I can't thank you all enough. You're family. Thank you for being family.

I'd also like to thank the townsfolk of both Paonia and Durango, where this cookbook was dually written. And Ed... Thanks for being an inspiration Ed.

And thank you for holding Wake & Bake: a cookbook in your loving hands. We're so glad you're part of this now.

RECIPE INDEX

Apple Crisp.. 55

Baked Biscuits.. 26

Bullseye Mashed Tater Egg Bake...................... 27

Chili Chocolate Cupcakes.................................... 43

Chocolate for Survival Frosting.......................... 82

Choose Your Own Adventure Chocolates........ 87

Cinnamon Rollies... 20

Conversion Chart.. 92

Cookie Dough Bites.. 49

Cornbread Brefas.. 24

Eggs in Some Basket... 31

Ethel's Sweede Pie... 57

Fake Bake Carrot Cake Muffins........................ 33

Faker Quaker Baker... 22

French Toast Casserole... 19

Fudge Nuggets.. 61

Ganashish.. 84

Ganja Flapjacks... 17

Green Drank.. 75

Green Monsta Oil... 6

Herb n Herb Nut Cheeze..................................... 68

High Chai (the resourceful way)........................ 9

High Chai Frosting.. 81

Highly Evolved Creamer....................................... 76

Hippie Speedball Creamer................................... 77

Hippie Speedball Smoothie................................. 78

Johnny Appleseed Muffins................................... 34

Merit Badge Cookies... 46

Mile High Muffins.. 36

Mothalovin' Pumpkin Pie...................................... 58

Nanner Muffins.. 38

No Bake Nut Butter Cookies............................... 51

Not Normal Chocolates... 90

PB Cups.. 89

Peanut Butter Sriracha Frosting......................... 83

Pot Tarts.. 18

Potcorn... 67

Pothead Pesto.. 69

Revolutionary Chocolate Cupcakes................... 41

Ripped Rice Crispy Pie.. 56

Roasted Veggie Quiche Meditation.................. 28

Seedy Truffles... 88

Shake n Bake Granola.. 14

Snickerdooodles... 45

Special Brownie Bites.. 62

Stooooonie Crisp Cereal...................................... 12

Sweet Tater Fry Bread.. 64

Tahini Maple Sugar Cookies............................... 52

Thank you.. 93

The Classic c3.. 48

The Dirty Hippie Shake... 72

The Doc Bronner Hippie Shake.......................... 73

The Trust Fund Hippie Shake.............................. 71

Thoughtless Cupcakes.. 42

Thumbprint Cookies... 50

Tortillas.. 30

Vavavanilla Icing.. 85

Weedies... 11

NOTES

ABOUT THE AUTHOR

Corinne Tobias is a writer, yoga teacher and an Organic Farmer Trophy Wife in training. One day, she will be completely focused on going to hot springs, hiking, growing flowers and melons, baking, traveling, and taking pictures of food... and she'll do it all in yoga pants. She's passionate about health and wellness, national marijuana reform, comedy, and overhauling the food system. She lives in Durango, CO. This is her first book.

ABOUT THE DESIGNER

Aja Kolinski is a graphic designer and artist out of Denver, Colorado. She's passionate about functional design, cannabis culture, her cat Mango and her dogs, Pebbles and Minnie. This is also her first book.

Made in the USA
Lexington, KY
26 April 2017